THE STORY OF THE
THEATRE

DAVID MALE

A & C·BLACK LTD
LONDON

Black's Junior Reference Books

General Editor R. J. Unstead

Published by A & C Black (Publishers) Limited, 35 Bedford Row, London WC1R 4JH

Reprinted 1982

ISBN 0-7136-0117-5

Second edition published 1967
Reprinted 1969, 1972, 1977, 1982
© 1967 A & C Black (Publishers) Limited

Printed in Great Britain by BAS Printers Limited, Over Wallop, Stockbridge, Hampshire.

CONTENTS

THE MARBLE PILLARS OF THE PARTHENON

ABOUT THIS BOOK

I wonder if you realise that plays were first performed more than two thousand years ago.

The purpose of this book is to tell you about the history of the theatre, from the time when plays were first acted in the theatres of ancient Greece. You can learn about the Roman circus, the wandering players of the Middle Ages, the miracle plays, the Elizabethan theatre, music halls, pantomime, cinema and television.

The word " theatre " covers many subjects and in this book you will find out about the men who wrote the plays and the actors and actresses who performed them, about costumes, make-up, scenery, " props " and lighting. The final chapter describes the popular " theatre " of today— television.

DAVID MALE

The Acropolis of Athens

1. THE THEATRES OF ANCIENT GREECE AND ROME

ANCIENT GREECE

To begin our story of the Theatre we have to travel a long way back into the past. Nearly five hundred years before Julius Caesar's expedition to Britain, there were theatres where actors performed well-known plays. To find them we should have to leave Britain, then a wild uncivilised country, cross most of the continent of Europe, and sail through the Mediterranean Sea, until we came to the country of Greece.

How different this country is from Britain. Rugged mountains rear up into the blue sky, and the hot sun beats down on us as we walk through the streets of the city of Athens. There are beautiful buildings and fine statues. High on a hill in the centre of the city, we can see a wonderful temple called the Parthenon.

If we could visit the boys at work in their schoolrooms, we should find them busy learning long poems and stories about famous Greek heroes.

Any Athenian schoolboy could recite at least part of the story of Odysseus, telling of his bravery during the Trojan War and his adventurous return home. Reciting was considered a great art. One famous reciter was said to know the whole

An Athenian boy learning his part

5

Learning to play the flute

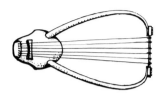

A Lyre

story of Odysseus by heart, and in really exciting parts " his eyes watered and his hair stood on end ".

Other boys would be having singing lessons or learning to play the flute or the lyre. Some would be learning to dance. The most popular was a war dance in which they imitated fighting with a spear and javelin. Dancing was a very important lesson, for sometimes the boys had the honour of dancing at a military parade, or in a procession to the temple of one of the Greek gods.

The Greeks had many gods and they worshipped them by singing long poems in their honour, performing special dances that told stories about the god or goddess and making sacrifices at the altar in the temple. It was at the temple of one of these gods that the story of the theatre really began.

A Choral Dance

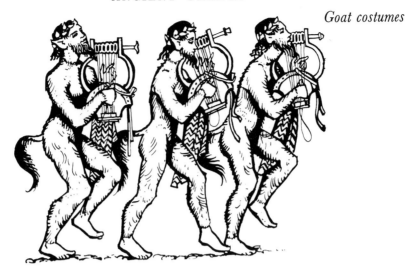

Goat costumes

Dionysus was a god of Nature. He was thought to die every autumn after the harvest of grapes had been gathered, and to be born again in the spring when the fresh buds appeared. Each spring a great festival was held in his honour.

Choral songs were sung or chanted, and dances were performed telling the story of the god. From these songs and dances the first plays were made. At first there was just one actor who spoke to the leader of the chorus. Later there were two actors who spoke to each other, while the chorus listened, or told part of the story.

As the years passed, the festival in honour of Dionysus became a festival at which plays were performed. Well-known stories of the gods, of heroes, or of the Trojan wars were acted. The audience knew the legends by heart and were curious to hear how well the poet told them.

Most of the plays written for the festival were called "tragedies". That is to say, they were sad stories that told of war, death or suffering. The word "tragedy" means "goat-song". No one is quite certain why this word was used. Some think it was because the chorus in procession to the temple wore goatskins, others think that the goat was given as a prize. Certainly prizes were given to the writer of the play voted to be the best.

All the boys working in the school-room hoped that they would be selected to act in one of the plays because it was a very great honour.

Voting for the best play

An Early Greek Theatre

THE GREEK THEATRE

Suppose that we are going to see one of these plays. The play begins very early in the morning. Nearly everyone in the city sets out for the theatre before sunrise, for no one in Athens works during the festival.

We find the theatre in the open on a hillside near the temple of Dionysus. The slope has been made into terraces with wooden or stone seats stretching round in a great half-circle. The flat space at the bottom of the slope, with a small altar in the middle, is called the " orchestra " which means " dancing place ".

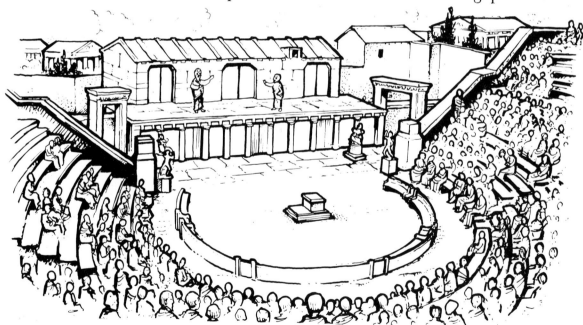

When the citizens of Athens and other Greek towns began to take a pride in their theatres, the rough wooden constructions of the early Greek theatres were replaced by fine buildings with pillars and arches of stone.

*The Chorus
in the Orchestra*

Behind this is a long low platform backed by a wooden building called the " skene ". Leading on to the platform from the " skene " is a large doorway, with smaller doors on either side.

At the moment it is too dark for us to see clearly, but as the sun slowly climbs over the horizon, the play begins.

High on the roof of the " skene " we see a watchman. He is looking for a signal bonfire telling him that the war against Troy is won and that the king will be returning home. The rising sun gives the effect of a beacon and the sentry excitedly shouts down the news of victory to the Queen in the palace below.

Now a group of about fifteen men, the " chorus ", move on to the " orchestra " space, performing a solemn dance and chanting aloud. They tell of the long and bitter Trojan War.

Then the great middle door at the back of the platform opens, and a strange figure, seeming to be about seven feet tall and wearing a large face mask, walks on to the stage. It is the Queen.

The Queen

The arrival of the King

The leader of the chorus asks her for news. She does not answer but makes a sacrifice to the god Apollo. Then she tells them of the victory. A herald brings further news of the battle. Later, the King appears in triumph, riding in a chariot, surrounded by his soldiers. He brings a captive from Troy who has warned the King that great dangers are ahead. But, heedless, he goes into the palace. A great cry is heard. The King has been murdered. The Queen had been plotting against him while he was away at the wars.

So the play goes on. We hear how the King's death is avenged, and the Queen punished. Altogether it takes several hours for the whole grim story to be acted.

THE ACTORS

If we could have a closer look at one of the actors, we should find out why he looks so tall. His shoes have very thick soles and tall heels. The hair of the mask covering his face is set in a special way to increase his height. The long, flowing robes that he wears are padded out so that he does not look too thin for his height.

The masks have been made to look like the different characters in the play. By using different masks the same actor can act two or three parts in a play. (This changing of masks is done because only three actors are allowed in one play.)

A hole is left in the mouth of the mask for the actor to speak through. It is shaped like a small megaphone to help the actor's voice reach the

Mouthpiece of mask

Three masks : A Flatterer, a Slave and a Hero

audience sitting a long way from the stage. The masks themselves help the audience to recognise each character from a distance.

Similar masks are still used today by Chinese actors, and the masks that are worn on Guy Fawkes Day or at Carnival time have been copied from the masks used by the Greeks.

Some of the processions to the temple of Dionysus were very much like carnivals. Crowds of townsfolk joined in the throng and enjoyed themselves. Songs in praise of Dionysus were sung, and people in fancy dress moved among the crowd joking and perhaps acting little scenes. There was great fun and much laughter.

At the temple a sacrifice was made and a grand final song chanted. It was from these processions that funny plays, plays to amuse people, began. They were called " comedies ". A long and serious " tragedy " was usually followed by a " comedy " at the festival of plays.

A procession to the Temple of Dionysus

Having seen the actor and his masks, we can now look at the stage itself. The platform is not very high and is rather narrow. Steps lead on to it from the " orchestra ". The large middle door at the back of the platform is used as the entrance to the King's palace. Behind the stage inside the " skene ", we may find some simple scenery, and also the " sound effects ". Here are some large jars filled with stones, standing near a big brass pot. This is the thunder machine. When thunder is required, the stones are poured into the pot to make as much noise as possible.

Lightning and thunder machines

The picture shows you what the " lightning " machine looks like. It is spun round to make one flash

The " eccylema " or trolley used on the stage to show the body of a person who had been killed

appear quickly after another. We also find a large trolley big enough for someone to lie on. This is used to show the body of a person who has been killed. It is pushed out on to the stage for the audience to see. The body of the murdered King was shown in this way. In Greek plays no " killing " could take place in front of the audience.

Sometimes, gods, or a messenger from Mount Olympus where the gods lived, appeared in plays. Instead of entering the stage through the doors, they were lowered by a rope from the top of the " skene " building.

No doubt the audience in the Greek theatre were thrilled when they saw a messenger from Olympus drop swiftly to the stage at an exciting point in the play, perhaps to aid one of the heroes who had prayed for help.

How different a visit to the Greek theatre seems from a visit to an English theatre of today! Yet, it is from the Greeks that the story of the theatre, which stretches over more than two thousand years, begins.

The plays of ancient Greece are still acted today, and we use the Greek names for parts of the theatre. The word " orchestra " meaning the dancing space in front of the stage is the name now given to the musicians who sit in that place in the theatre or concert hall. The building called the " skene " has given us the word " scenery ". The

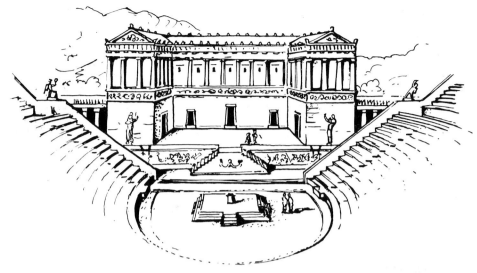

A Roman Theatre

" skene " was first used to represent the royal palace in a play, and later was used as a store for scenery and a place where the actors could change their costumes. The word " chorus " means a group of people singing or speaking together.

THE ROMAN THEATRE

When the Romans became a great power they built theatres on a plan copied from the Greeks. They used Greek stories. Even the costumes worn by the Roman actors were copied from Greek stage costumes. Many years later during the Middle Ages, we find actors in Italy using masks very similar to the Greek ones.

If you visit Italy or South France, you can still see some of the theatres built by the Romans on the Greek plan. There are also the remains of a Roman theatre at St. Albans, Hertfordshire.

These theatres were richly decorated with fine carvings and beautiful statues. It is said that sometimes the seats were sprinkled with rose-water to make the air smell sweet.

A comic actor   *A tragic actor*

A mock sea-battle

The Romans borrowed Greek plays to act. They preferred the amusing comedies that made them laugh, so the Roman poets wrote plays of a similar sort. Playgoing was very popular and many fine theatres were built.

These large Roman theatres made suitable arenas for the circus displays the Romans enjoyed so much. In intervals during the plays, the audience could watch acrobatic tricks, juggling, dancing and performing animals. These "interludes" became more popular than the plays, and they were made even more spectacular by horse shows, battling gladiators and animal baiting.

The " orchestra " of one theatre was made into a miniature lake and a naval battle fought out by small sailing ships. Eager Roman citizens clamoured for more and more excitement and the performances in specially built " amphitheatres " became cruel displays, where, as well as the popular gladiatorial combats, the audience would watch wild animals being let loose among helpless slaves and captives. This evil practice ceased only when a Christian Emperor took command.

Italian masks

Gladiators

Mediaeval strolling players : a Minstrel, a Dancer, a boy Juggler and two Tumblers

2. PLAYERS AND PLAYS IN THE MIDDLE AGES

When Rome was attacked by the barbarians from Germany, cities and theatres fell into decay. The poems and plays of the Greeks and Romans were lost and forgotten for hundreds of years.

STROLLING PLAYERS

Some of the actors, dancers and circus entertainers took to a wandering life, and continued to act their little plays, or give juggling performances and acrobatic displays wherever they could find an audience.

For hundreds of years, these performances were the only kind of " theatre " that existed. Wandering players travelled the countries of Europe, stopping here and there on a village green or in the market square of a town. Often they performed before lords and ladies in their castles.

The minstrels, dressed in brightly coloured costumes, sang songs about battles and heroes, while acrobats gave dancing or tumbling displays.

A Bagpiper and an Organ-player

There were also puppet masters who presented little plays acted by roughly carved wooden marionettes.

The strolling players gave a performance wherever a crowd gathered, as it did on holidays such as May Day when the country folk danced round the Maypole. This was a tall be-ribboned post decorated with spring flowers and leaves.

During the autumn, some towns held great trade fairs. One of the largest was at Stourbridge, where row upon row of market stalls was set up. Buyers and sellers haggled to get good prices for woollen cloth, salted fish, leather parchment and goods of every kind.

At these great Michaelmas Fairs, which drew country and townsfolk

A Puppet Show

from miles around, knots of open-mouthed villeins watched the conjuror's mysterious tricks while his companion cut their purse strings; they crowded to see the juggler with his knives and balls, the rope-walkers and fire-eaters, while the minstrels sang and the gleemen banged merrily on drum and pipe.

The Conjuror and the Fire-eater

A Village May Day

Kings and noblemen kept a minstrel or joker living at their courts to entertain their friends and visitors. At the Battle of Hastings, William the Conqueror's minstrel, Tallifer,

> " who famed for song,
> Mounted on a charger strong,
> Rode before the Duke and sang
> Of Roland and Charlemagne "

was still singing and twirling his sword, as he led the Norman charge and died in front of the Saxon shield-wall.

Blondel

When Richard I was captured, his minstrel, Blondel, is said to have discovered his master's place of captivity by singing a favourite song outside many a castle, until an answering voice told him where the imprisoned king lay.

An Easter Play

PLAYS IN CHURCH

Few people, even kings, could read and write. In church, the priest spoke Latin which the ordinary people in the congregation could not understand.

To make the Easter Day service more easily understood, a little play was acted. The altar of the church was used as the tomb where Jesus was buried. Three priests, dressed as the women going to anoint the body of Jesus, walked to the tomb. They were met by two more priests dressed as angels.

A Christmas Play

"Whom do you seek in the tomb?" they chant.

"We are looking for Jesus who was crucified," the women reply.

The angels give their strange, yet wonderful answer. "He is not here, He has arisen."

Then the women turn to the choir and announce, "Hallelujah! The Lord has arisen!"

They search in the tomb and find the linen clothes, showing that the body has gone. Then the priest begins a hymn of praise and the church bells are rung, proclaiming the good news.

As the years passed, other stories about Jesus were acted at the services. At Christmas the villagers could watch the shepherds and the three Kings journeying to see the baby Jesus in the stable. The priests and the choirboys were the actors.

Different parts of the church were used to represent Galilee, Pilate's Palace, Herod's Court, Heaven and Hell, in the Christmas and Easter plays. These special places were called "mansions".

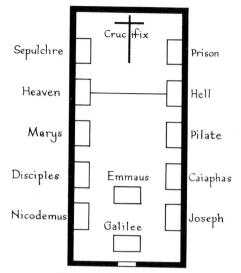

Sepulchre — Cruxifix — Prison

Heaven — Hell

Marys — Pilate

Disciples — Emmaus — Caiaphas

Nicodemus — Galilee — Joseph

Plan of the " Mansions "

So many people came to see the plays that the church became crowded. Then the plays were performed outside the church doors. The priests became worried lest the plays were getting too noisy, and the people more interested in watching them than in worshipping God. The priests began to take a smaller part in producing these plays.

GILD PLAYS

Instead of the plays being acted in the churchyard, they were performed on carts called " pageants " in the square or streets of the town. Craftsmen and workers, such as the tanners, dyers, weavers and carpenters, belonged to clubs called " gilds ", and the acting of the plays was taken over by the members of the various craft-gilds, probably encouraged by the clergy.

Many stories from the Bible were made into plays until, in time, the whole story of the Bible from " Adam " to " The Last Judgement " was being acted.

On the special feast day of " Corpus Christi ", which is soon after Whitsuntide, a whole " cycle ", or group of plays, would be acted. All day long the streets were crowded with people keen to see these " Mystery " plays as they were called.

Mediaeval plays were acted on carts called " pageants "

Let us imagine that we are among that holiday crowd and find out what really happens.

The day before the feast, the town-crier has gone round the town warning people to behave themselves next day, and to leave their swords and other weapons at home.

A good place to watch is at the town gate. We must be there early to get a good view. The plays begin soon after sunrise. A "pageant" carrying the actors stops on the open space in front of the gates.

The Town-Crier

" Adam and Eve " Pageant

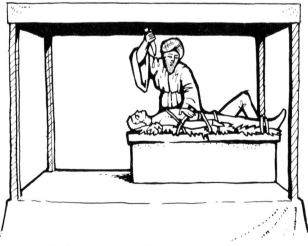

" Abraham and Isaac " Pageant

This cart is two storeys high, with a curtain enclosing the lower part, where the actors put on their costumes. A wooden roof covers the upper level which is decorated with flowers and leaves to look like the Garden of Eden. It is open at the sides and front, so that everyone can see the actors. The story of Adam and Eve and the wicked serpent is acted by the Drapers' Gild.

When the scene ends, the cart moves off to the next stopping place, or "station", in the town. We wait eagerly for the next cart to arrive. All day the procession goes on.

We see the story of Noah acted by the water-carriers of the town, on a cart built to look like a ship. We watch Isaac about to be sacrificed by Abraham.

" The Shepherds " Pageant

Herod

Altogether, there may be thirty or forty scenes performed. Some of them are quite amusing. In the play about the shepherds, we see Mac taking home a stolen sheep. When the shepherds come to look for it, Mac's wife puts it into a cradle and pretends that it is her baby.

We watch Herod raging because the Wise Men have not returned to him. So great is his rage that he leaves the platform and stamps up and down the street.

Most exciting perhaps is the cart made to look like " Hell ". It is shaped like a huge dragon's mouth. Real smoke and flames burst out from it. Lucifer (the Devil) himself appears, and his many assistants, who dart among the crowds. These devils are very ugly to look at but they make us laugh. They are dressed as wolves or rams with great horns or bells on their heads.

Lucifer and his Devils

We see the actor playing *Jesus* hanging on a real wooden cross. An old French manuscript tells how a priest playing the part of *Jesus* in the Crucifixion scene, fainted and nearly died from the pain he suffered.

One by one the scenes are acted, until by evening we have watched the whole story of the Bible, and another *Corpus Christi* holiday is over.

The Crucifixion

The " Stations " in the streets of a town

Different groups of craftsmen each produced one scene. They nearly always chose a scene that had something to do with their own particular job. In York for example, the Shipwrights' Gild produced the play about Noah and the Ark ; the barbers acted the scene about John the Baptist, and the goldsmiths naturally took the parts of the Three Kings.

Each gild would build up its own pageant, and provide the actors. Young apprentices took part, and received some reward for their efforts. An old parchment at Coventry tells how the actor playing Herod received 3s. 4d., Pontius Pilate 4s., the Devil and Judas 1s. 6d.

Acting must have been a very thirsty job because the list also tells us that nine gallons of ale costing 1s. 6d. were provided, as well as a rib of beef and one goose costing 6d. The players would certainly need refreshment after acting all day.

Although the carts were rough, the actors were gaudily dressed. The actor playing God wore a coat of white leather, with a white beard and wig. The list also mentioned scarlet gowns, silk fringes, gloves, hats and caps.

We find a payment for hemp to repair the angels' wings, and 8d. paid for painting their wings. A list from Norwich mentions :

A cote & hosen for Adam steyned
A cote wt hosen and tayle for ye serpente steyned, wt a wt heare

"Steyned" means "stained" or "dyed", and "heare" a wig. "Hosen" were tight fitting trousers.

There was only one copy of the play, and this was carefully preserved. All the instructions telling the actors what to do and say were written on it. There are still copies of these old plays from a number of towns in England. The most famous are those at Coventry, Chester, Wakefield and York. The forty-eight plays from the York "cycle" have been translated into modern English and performed in York.

The York Mystery Plays : a modern production in York

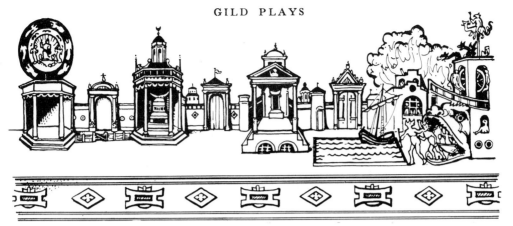

A Mediaeval Stage in a town square in France or Germany

In Germany, at the village of Oberammergau, the Passion, or Crucifixion, plays are still performed, with the villagers as the actors. Thousands of people flock to see these plays that have existed ever since the Middle Ages.

In France and Germany the plays were not acted on carts, but on a long platform set up in the town square. The picture shows different " mansions " stretched out in a long line with " Heaven " at one end and " Hell " at the other.

The jaws of " Hell " really opened and closed. Real smoke and flames were made by burning pitch. Ugly masked devils with pitchforks clambered out to get their victims. The audience must have felt quite frightened, especially when the " devils " left the stage and came among them, and they heard the shrieks and moans coming from inside the monster's mouth.

MORALITY PLAYS

Besides the " mysteries " and " miracles ", there were plays called " moralities ". In these, the actors did not have parts like Noah, Herod or Judas, but were called " Death ", " Good-deeds ", " Beauty " or " Strength ". The actors represented the kind or selfish thoughts of a person.

Masks for the Devils

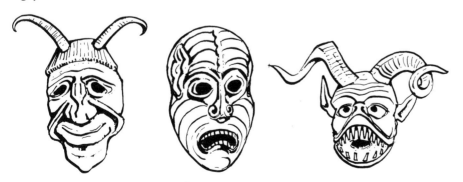

A scene from " Everyman "

The best known morality play is *Everyman*, which tells how a man is called by Death to go on a journey to God.

He appeals to his friends for help, but they all find excuses for not going.

" I've got cramp in my toe ", says one of his relations.

" Go and ask a priest to help you," says Knowledge.

Beauty will not go with him for all the gold in his chest.

Only Good-deeds will accompany him. He says :

" I will go with thee and be thy guide,

In thy most need to go by thy side."

In Aesop's Fables you will remember that each story has a moral, pointing out the need to be kind, gentle or unselfish. These "Morality" plays did the same thing.

Through the Middle Ages until the sixteenth century these various kinds of plays were performed. They were plays in which the whole town joined, either as actors or audience.

It was a time for holiday enjoyment, excited bustling crowds, laughter at the comic scenes.

In the play called *The Deluge*, telling about the Flood, Noah argued fiercely with his wife because she would not leave her gossiping friends, to go into the Ark. When at last she was heaved in, she gave Noah a slap for his pains.

A scene from " The Deluge "

The man who played "The Ass"

Yet it was a serious festival as well. The people were reminded in a very vivid way of the story of Christ's birth, life, death and resurrection.

OTHER FESTIVALS

Not quite so serious was another feast called *The Feast of the Ass*. At first, Bible stories were acted in which a donkey appeared. But later, rather vulgar fun was made of the church services and priests. Although this display disappeared after some years because the church disapproved, the idea of a comic man wearing ass's ears remained.

A monk studying a manuscript

Another ceremony was known as *The Festival of the Boy Bishop*. The chief choirboy of the cathedral was elected "Bishop" for a short time. He was dressed in Bishop's robes and treated with great respect. During this two-week holiday, there was dancing and play-acting.

Perhaps you have taken part in, or watched, a "Nativity" play in your own church or school. These Christmas plays are very much like the Mystery plays acted in church during the Middle Ages.

The story of the theatre in the Middle Ages is a mixture of minstrels, acrobats, sword dancers, plays in church and plays in the market square. For the most part the plays of that time were Bible stories or stories of saints. The craftsmen, goldsmiths, painters, fishmongers, bakers, their journeymen and young apprentices were the players.

Children in a school Nativity Play

Plays were often performed in innyards

3. SHAKESPEARE AND THE " GLOBE "

PLAYS IN INNYARDS

The Miracle and Mystery plays were very popular, but they were only acted once or twice each year. People enjoyed watching plays so much, that they gave a ready welcome to the strolling players, minstrels and other wandering actors who banded together into " professional " companies. These moved from town to town acting little plays called " interludes ".

When the strolling players came to a town, they first went to the Mayor to obtain his permission to hold their show. Then, one or two of the company paraded through the streets with trumpet and drum, announcing to all and sundry that a play was about to be performed in the innyard. Meanwhile the landlord, pleased to welcome extra customers, had barrels dragged out into the courtyard and planks laid across them to make the stage.

Spectators, who paid a penny each, pushed and elbowed each other in the courtyard to get a good position to see the play. Portly merchants and their wives, town councillors and well-to-do tradesmen watched from the balconies that

28

Announcing the play

surrounded the open courtyard. Usually the "interludes" were amusing.

In one, four men had a competition to see who could tell the biggest lie. In another, the characters were given a chance to choose what weather they would like. One wanted sunshine, another demanded rain for the crops. In fact there was so much argument that the "Clerk of the Weather" decided to carry on with the usual mixture.

To us these little plays would seem rather rough and ready, with long-winded speeches and a good deal of clowning. But the innyard audience enjoyed them immensely, cheering the hero and shouting out rude remarks if the play did not please them.

Unfortunately the actors were still thought of as ruffians and vagabonds.

They could be whipped or chased out of town unless they were under the protection of some nobleman or lord. So we hear of "The Earl of Leicester's Men", "The Lord Admiral's Men" or "The Lord Chamberlain's Men".

Noblemen's Coats of Arms, worn by groups of players

The Earl of Worcester's Arms

The Earl of Warwick's Arms

The Duke of Somerset's Arms

PLANS IN COURT AND COLLEGE

Rather more dignified performances were given in the homes of rich noblemen or courtiers, and in the colleges at Oxford and Cambridge. A platform stage would be built at one end of the hall, and a richly dressed, educated audience would gather for an evening's entertainment. Perhaps an interlude would be acted, or one of the old Roman plays would be brought back to the stage after lying forgotten for hundreds of years.

A Play in a College Hall

Boys at Choir schools attached to some cathedrals were trained to act in plays. The "Children of the Royal Chapel" became very famous for their acting in the reign of Queen Elizabeth I. In fact, some of the grown-up actors became quite jealous of the boys' success.

Boys also performed with the professional companies, acting the women's parts, as women were not allowed to appear on the stage in public.

LONDON'S FIRST THEATRES

In 1576, the very first theatre appeared in London. It was called the "Theatre", built by James Burbage at a cost of about £700. Soon, another named the "Curtain" was built nearby. Both theatres were extremely popular, except with the Puritans who did not approve of play-acting. It was also feared that people crowding together to watch a play would help spread the dreadful disease called the Plague. To avoid trouble, the theatres were built outside the city where the Lord Mayor could not interfere so easily.

The Globe Theatre

On the south bank of the River Thames was Bankside, famous for its pleasure gardens, low taverns and popular shows. Here the Londoners came to watch animal-baiting, when a bear and sometimes a bull or an ape was fastened to a post and attacked by fierce dogs. These cruel sports attracted large crowds, and it was at Bankside that several more theatres were built. Most famous were the "Rose" and the "Swan", and, best known of all, the "Globe".

THE "GLOBE"

Let us join the bustling crowds hurrying across London Bridge, or being ferried across the river by boatmen on a fine afternoon. The roof of the "Globe" is just in sight and we are glad to see the flag fluttering from the tower. Now we know for certain that a play will be performed today. Impatiently we hurry through Bankside, straining our ears to catch the sound of the trumpet which tells us that the play is about to begin.

At last we are there. We push our way through the narrow doorway, pay our penny entrance money and scramble to find a good place to stand and watch the play.

We are standing in an open courtyard called the "pit", among the noisy apprentices and workmen who are known as the "groundlings". As we look round, we can see that the "Globe" is not so very different from an innyard "theatre".

The trumpet announces that the play is about to begin

In front of us is a large platform called an "apron" stage, because it projects into the audience, and behind us are the galleries where for 2d. and 3d. we could have a more comfortable seat, sheltered from the rain.

Those dashing young noblemen, whom you see laughing and joking as they sit on the stage itself, have paid a shilling or more for their seats. There in full view of the audience they can show off their fine clothes, and criticise the play and its author.

To pass the time before the play begins, these young "gallants" often play cards or indulge in the new-fashioned habit of smoking tobacco.

While we are waiting, we can quench our dry throats with ale or wine, or buy apples, pears and nuts

Inside the Globe Theatre

from the noisy pedlars who shoulder their way among the groundlings, bawling their wares and holding up baskets of fruit.

Looking again at the stage, we see two tall pillars rising from it to support a small roof. The under side of the roof is painted with the sun, moon, and stars to look like the sky.

Any gods, goddesses, or messengers from the " Heavens " will be let down on a rope from a trapdoor in the roof.

Behind the apron stage is an inner stage or " chamber ". This is used for scenes taking place indoors, perhaps in a bedroom or a monk's cell. Curtains can be drawn to hide it from the audience's view.

The roof over the stage

Above the chamber we can see a balcony which may serve as the battlements of a castle, the high walls of a town or even as the bridge of a ship. Here we might also find the musicians, trumpeters and drummers ready to sound a fanfare heralding the approach of a king or prince.

Also in the tower part of the theatre are the " sound effects " men. Their job is to produce the sound of cannons firing, thunder rumbling and flashes. One story says that the first " Globe " theatre was burnt down because of an over-enthusiastic cannon firer. Luckily everyone escaped safely, except one poor man whose trousers caught alight. But someone quenched that blaze with a glass of ale.

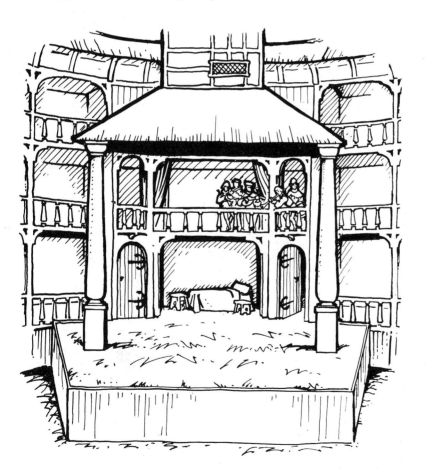

The Chamber and Balcony

The Chorus

The trumpeter is climbing into the little balcony beside the tower. He sounds a fanfare. The play is about to begin.

We are going to see an exciting play about King Henry V and his battles with the King of France. An actor called the " Chorus " (Story-teller) comes through one of the entrances on either side of the apron stage, and walks forward.

" Imagine," he says, " that this round theatre holds the vast battle-fields of France. When we see one soldier, we must think of him as a thousand. When there is talk of horses, we must pretend to hear and see their clattering hoofs."

A Scene from " Henry V." The Siege of Harfleur

The story unfolds. The English army lays siege to the French town of Harfleur. High up from the tower we hear the sound of cannons and trumpets urging the soldiers to battle. King Henry strides forward to encourage his men.

Four or five soldiers with scaling ladders swarm up on to the balcony which represents the wall of the city. Fierce combat follows, and at last the English are victorious.

All in the audience are thrilled. The groundlings have enjoyed the blood and thunder of the battle scenes, and laughed at some comic soldiers who argued and quarrelled among themselves instead of fighting. The more respectable citizens in the boxes and balconies, as well as the young gallants, preferred the fine poetic speeches and the retelling of a brave episode in English history.

WILLIAM SHAKESPEARE

William Shakespeare

Henry V was written by a young man named William Shakespeare whose plays were becoming very popular. As a boy, Shakespeare lived at Stratford-on-Avon in Warwickshire. His father was a glove maker and butcher, and by all accounts William was a very lively lad.

He was very fond of the streams and meadows of Warwickshire and,

it is said, also enjoyed trapping and poaching rabbits from the local squire's estate. One story says that he had to leave Stratford because he had been caught trying to poach a deer from Sir Thomas Lucy's estate, but this may not be true.

As a young man he went to London. Being very keen on the Theatre, he found a job with the Lord Chamberlain's Men. At first he was the odd-job boy, calling the actors when they were needed or holding the carriage horses.

One of Shakespeare's first jobs

The Royal Shakespeare Theatre, Stratford-on-Avon

Then he became an actor, and later still began to write plays himself. Many of these plays were performed at the " Globe " Theatre with an actor named Richard Burbage taking the chief parts. (Richard's father had built the " Globe ".)

William Shakespeare became very famous. Even Queen Elizabeth I became interested in his plays. We know that he and Burbage performed at her Court at Greenwich, and that he also wrote a play called *The Merry Wives of Windsor* at her command, in which he made fun of a magistrate said to be the Sir Thomas Lucy who had punished him for poaching.

Shakespeare's plays are still acted today. A special theatre has been built at Stratford-on-Avon. Each year thousands of people from all parts of the world go to see plays such as *Henry V, Hamlet, A Midsummer Night's Dream* or others of the many plays he wrote.

SCENERY AND COSTUMES

The " Globe " was very different from a modern theatre. It was open to the wind and rain. The actors pretended that various parts of the stage were different places without any change of scenery. Either the " Chorus " told us where the scene was taking place, or we had to wait until the actors told us in one of their speeches.

A Forest Scene from " As You Like It "

Sometimes a bush in a barrel might represent a forest, or a notice was displayed saying " A street in Venice " or " The King's Palace ". Plays could not take place at night because of the difficulty and danger of lighting the theatre.

But if the scenery was poor and stage-lighting entirely absent, the costumes at the " Globe " were splendid enough. There were also stage costumes which we should find amusing but which everyone understood and accepted.

In plays about the Romans, for instance, Roman armour was worn over Elizabethan dress. Characters from Eastern lands dressed more realistically, they had long, flowing costumes and turbans. Another strange garment was " the robe to go invisible in ". When an actor wore this, the others pretended they could not see him.

PLAYERS AND PLAYS

The companies of actors working in Bankside playhouses continued to be very popular except with the Puritans, who were always trying to close the theatres and prevent new ones being built. When a rival acting company tried to open a new theatre called the " Fortune ", in 1600, they were only successful because Queen Elizabeth overruled the Puritan Lord Mayor.

Acting, however, was still a risky way of earning a living. The players received no regular wages. Instead, they were paid a share of the theatre takings. If the theatre was closed because of plague or bad weather the actors had to manage as best they could.

A Roman Soldier

A Moorish Captain

A Scene from " The Tempest "

The audiences were always eager to see new plays so the writers were kept very busy, often altering old plays or retelling well-known stories. Perhaps they might be paid a few pounds for their efforts, or given a share in the profit from their play.

You can imagine the anxious author wandering about the " tiring house " behind the stage, straining his ears to hear if the audience were clapping or hissing his play, for the groundlings showed their feelings very plainly. Marlowe, Shakespeare and Ben Jonson were some of those who were busy writing exciting plays.

Stories of some of the famous kings and queens in history were made into plays. So were stories of daring soldiers and adventurers. When the plays told sad tales of death or revenge, they were called "tragedies". Others called "comedies" made the audience laugh. Boasting soldiers, country yokels, clowns and practical jokers got up to all kinds of tricks.

In one play called *The Tempest*, two clowns crawl under a large blanket so that only their feet are showing, and someone coming in thinks it is a dreadful monster.

In *A Midsummer Night's Dream*, a mischievous fairy named Puck captures a poor weaver called Bottom and disguises him as a donkey. He then scatters some magic juice on the Fairy Queen's eyes so that when she wakes, she thinks this donkey is

A Scene from " A Midsummer Night's Dream "

the most beautiful creature she has ever met and falls in love with him.

PRIVATE THEATRES

If you were a wealthy nobleman or a courtier at the Queen's Palace, you would not perhaps visit any of the "public" theatres. You would go to see a play at a "private" indoor theatre.

How different this is from the "Globe"! The stage is separated from us by an arch called the "proscenium" which is beautifully carved and painted. So that we can see the actors clearly, the stage is lit by candles. No need to imagine the scene here, for at the back of the stage is stretched a huge canvas cloth wonderfully painted to look like a sky with billowing clouds.

On either side are tall wooden screens covered with canvas, painted to represent the buildings of a city. More exciting still—the screens or "flats" as they are called, can be slid out of view when the scene ends. Other screens, representing a leafy orchard, are put in their place. In a few moments the scene is transformed from a street in a city to a grove in an apple orchard.

An architect named Inigo Jones brought these new ideas of painted and movable scenery to England from Italy. Often they were used for "Court Masques", which were splendid entertainments rather than

The Proscenium Arch and Stage of a Private Theatre

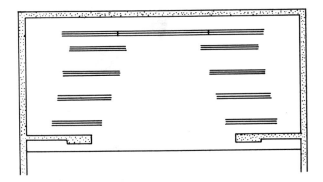

How the flats were arranged in a Private Theatre

plays. Queen Elizabeth and later King James I and Charles I were frequently entertained by masques written specially to please them.

These performances were usually arranged by a court official known as " Master of the Revels ". Young courtiers and ladies wearing rich and elaborate costumes danced to lilting music. Verses of poetry were spoken or sung. The beautifully painted scenery was brilliantly lit with hundreds of candles—altogether a marvellous and glittering sight.

The masque usually ended with a gift for the Queen, and a poem recited in praise of her. Nobles, seeking the Queen's favour, often presented a masque when she visited their home during one of her " progresses " through the kingdom.

During the reigns of Queen Elizabeth and the first Stuart kings, the theatres grew and flourished. Private indoor theatres were built at Blackfriars, Salisbury Court and at the " Cockpit " in Drury Lane.

Suddenly our story of the Theatre comes to an abrupt halt.

The quarrels between the King and Parliament became so great that, in 1642, civil war broke out. Parliament, consisting mainly of Puritans, was victorious. The Puritans did not approve either of theatres or actors and they believed that the performance of women's parts by boys was particularly wicked. Now at last these dens of evil could be closed and torn down.

No longer did the crowds swarm across London Bridge to see the newest play at the " Globe " or the " Swan ". Here and there, however, a few actors risked putting on a play despite the ban by Parliament.

A Puritan

4. INDOOR THEATRES

THE RESTORATION THEATRE

In 1660, amid the roar of welcoming cannons and pealing church bells, King Charles II was restored to the English throne and Puritan rule came to an end. Immediately the actors and managers who had been working secretly for several years, reopened the theatres. One manager, Sir William Davenant, had already managed to present a play with music, by cleverly disguising the fact that it was a play. He called it " music and instruction ".

The new king was very fond of play-going, and he gave permission for two acting companies to be formed in London. They were the " King's Men ", and the " Duke of York's Company ". Within a few years the King's Men moved into a new theatre in Drury Lane, and the rival company established themselves at a converted indoor tennis court in Lincoln's Inn Fields.

Luckily for us, Mr. Samuel Pepys, well known for his famous *Diary*,

King Charles II

was alive at this time. He was a very enthusiastic playgoer. In fact, he often went three or four times a week ! He is our guide to the " Royal Theatre " in Drury Lane.

AT DRURY LANE THEATRE

The performance takes place in the afternoon, and to be in the fashion we shall hire a boatman to row us down the river to the landing stage near the theatre. This fine playhouse cost nearly £2500 to build.

Mr. Samuel Pepys

Setting out for the theatre by boat

Inside a Restoration Theatre

Mr. Pepys has some friends in the acting company, so we have the privilege of going behind the scenes. In the " Tiring Rooms " (dressing-rooms) the players are busy putting on their beautiful costumes and colouring their faces with rouge and chalk. There are actresses as well as actors. The old law for-bidding women to appear on the public stage has been withdrawn.

Mr. Pepys is full of praise for an actress named Nell Gwyn, much admired for her beauty and skill in comedy parts. Nell started work at Drury Lane as an orange-seller, but speedily became one of the most popular actresses of the day.

Backstage, the scene shifters stack up the piles of " flats " needed for the different scenes in the play. We can see that many of Inigo Jones's ideas have been employed in this theatre. There are grooves for the flats to slide in and out. Other pieces of scenery are hauled out of sight above the stage by ropes and pulleys. A rich curtain separates us from the audience.

A candle-snuffer carefully lights the candles in the great chandeliers. Throughout the performance he will be on watch, ready to creep out and snuff any dangerously guttering candles.

The candle-snuffer

As the play is about to begin, Mr. Pepys takes us to his favourite seat in the pit. Looking about us we can see that in some ways this theatre is similar to the " Globe ". The stage still juts out into the pit where we are sitting on cloth-covered benches. The floor slopes up steeply towards the back where there are boxes, and galleries above, not unlike those of the Elizabethan Playhouse ; but the whole building is roofed in.

In the centre box sitting on a beautiful, gilded chair is King Charles II, with his courtiers. The " Merry Monarch " frequently comes to the theatre, and he is a great admirer of Nell Gwyn. Mr. Pepys is known

Nell Gwyn

to the King, and he fervently hopes that His Majesty will honour him with a smile or a nod.

How beautifully everyone in the audience is dressed ! Indeed, some only come to the theatre to show off their fine clothes and meet their friends. The ladies wear expensive linen or silk dresses.

Some, in the very latest fashion, hold masks in front of their faces to hide their identity. Much amusement is caused among the young gallants who delight in guessing who these coy ladies are. The boxes and the pit are full of courtiers, wealthy lords and ladies, or gay young men-about-town.

An orange-seller

their masters to the theatre, and stay to enjoy the play themselves.

An orange-seller entreats us to buy juicy oranges—only sixpence each. Mr. Pepys whispers to us to have a care what we pay. These lasses are not slow to give short change to the unwary customer.

Now an actor walks on to the fore-stage and speaks the prologue. He explains what the play is about, as well as making witty remarks about the audience. He begs them not to be too critical of the play and its author, and hopes they will enjoy what follows.

The curtain rises and the comedy begins.

Above the boxes in the galleries are the less expensive seats. Here we find the noisier members of the audience. The upper gallery is the favourite meeting-place of the coachmen and lackeys who have brought

The play begins

Changing the scenery while the play continues

The play tells of the exploits of a gay young courtier in love with a pretty young girl. Her doddering old aunt raises objections to the match. But with the help of some crafty servants she is outwitted.

There are some anxious moments when a letter gets into the wrong hands, and the plotters are overheard by a servant in the enemy camp. All, however, ends well. The courtly audience enjoy the witty remarks of the hero, and the fun poked at the old aunt.

In one play, Mr. Pepys tells us, some rather impudent remarks were made about the King. The audience enjoyed it but the King was extremely angry and forbade the play to be acted any more.

We are rather surprised to notice that when the scene ends, the stage shifters run on to the stage and change the set in full view of the audience. New flats are quickly placed in position. Meanwhile the actors move on to the fore-stage, and the swiftly changed scenery transports them from the young man's dressing room to St. James's Park.

At the end of Act I a " gatherer " comes round to collect our entrance fee of 2s. 6d. The custom is to take the money after the first act. If we do not like the play and want to leave we can do so without paying.

Some cunning members of the audience manage to dodge payment altogether by flitting between pit and gallery while the collector is on his rounds. The box-holders pay four shillings, and those in the

tainment. We then ride back to our lodging in a hired coach.

The chandeliers that illuminated the theatre were beautiful, but they were extremely dangerous. One evening in 1672 the Drury Lane Theatre became a blazing inferno. Fire completely destroyed all the scenery and costumes. Gunpowder was used to blow up the adjoining houses to prevent the blaze spreading. The damage amounted to many thousands of pounds. Undaunted, the manager, Thomas

The dancers in the Masque

gallery 1s. 6d. The very top gallery only costs a shilling. The King pays £10 for his box.

After the play, a Masque performed by French dancers accompanied by music from the little orchestra, concludes our enter-

Killigrew, began planning a new theatre with the help of the famous architect, Sir Christopher Wren.

SCENES AND MACHINES

Wren had already designed a handsome theatre for the Duke of York's Players at Dorset Gardens. Magnificent carving and statues decorated the inside of this theatre. The audience were delighted with the splendid new scenery painted by artists who had brought back the latest ideas from France and Italy. Views of pillared temples, groves of blossoming trees, harbours with sailing ships, enchanted the eye.

Returning home from the theatre by coach

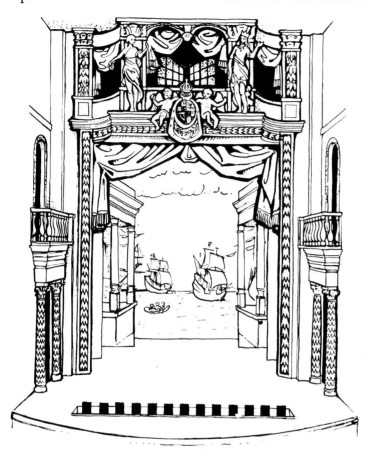

*The stage of the
Dorset Gardens
Theatre*

Pretty Cupids sailed down on
cloud machines drawn by peacocks,
while pyramids of fire glowed in
the background. Usually a play
was only performed three or four
times (more if it was a great success)
so the same scenery often appeared
in several different plays.

The poor over-worked actors must
have had a hard time continually
learning fresh parts. Most famous
among the actors was Thomas
Betterton. Samuel Pepys said, " He
is the best actor in the world ".

Cupids in a cloud machine

A Scene from Shakespeare's " Henry VIII ". Only the King and Wolsey are in Tudor costume

He was equally good in comic and serious parts, and was specially praised for his performances in revivals of Shakespeare's plays. These were often performed using the new, beautiful and spectacular scenic effects.

COSTUMES

Not quite so much care was taken with the actors' costumes. In a performance of *Henry VIII*, the King and Cardinal Wolsey were both dressed in their correct Tudor costumes. The rest of the actors wore court dress of a hundred years later. Sometimes the leading men actors tried to wear the appropriate costume, but the ladies preferred to wear dresses of their own period, even if they were acting the part of an ancient Egyptian.

Left: A " Roman " Costume in the Restoration Theatre

Right: An " Egyptian " Lady in the Restoration Theatre

A " Moorish Captain " in the Restoration Theatre

David Garrick as King Lear

Actors playing Eastern characters usually sported tall, plumed turbans, flowing, fur-edged coats and rather baggy trousers. In a play about the Romans some of the actors would wear Roman togas, while others dressed in the fashion of their own day. This sort of confusion did not seem to bother the Restoration audiences.

THE EIGHTEENTH AND NINETEENTH CENTURIES

As the years sped by, hundreds of plays, some good, others bad, were performed in London theatres. Disastrous theatre fires, fierce rivalry and quarrels between the actors, kept play-acting in the news. The delight in playgoing spread beyond the circle of courtiers and well-to-do. Merchants and shopkeepers now joined their ranks.

The audiences cheered and applauded great performers like David Garrick, Charles Macklin, Edmund Kean and Mrs. Sarah Siddons.

Mrs. Sarah Siddons as Lady Macbeth

John Kemble, another great Shakespearian actor, as Hamlet

" Cat-calls " in the theatre

They were not slow either in showing their disapproval with shouts and " cat-calls ". Rioters, encouraged by noisy rattles and clanging dustmen's bells, once clambered on to the stage at Drury Lane to protest against an increase in admission charge. One madman even tried to shoot King George III as he sat in the Royal Box.

A madman tries to shoot the King

During the eighteenth century an inventive young man named Loutherbourg produced some exciting lighting effects by placing coloured glass in front of the footlights, and lights placed at each side of the stage in the " wings ".

He also produced effects of blazing fire and volcanoes, as well as thunder and lightning. Loutherbourg also showed his talents as an artist with wonderful scenes of moorland, forest and rocky hilltops.

Gradually stage settings became more realistic. The position of the side flats was altered, so that they represented the actual walls of a room. They fitted together like three sides of a box.

Improved lighting in the " wings "
of the stage

Edmund Kean as Shylock

Edmund Kean, with the help of learned professors, searched old documents and drawings to make sure the costumes in his plays were historically correct. So that the audience should appreciate his hard work, Kean wrote a long note in the programme giving details of his investigations.

He even mentioned that the trees and plants painted on the scenery were those that grew in that part of the world where the scene was taking place. In some woodland scenes, you might find live rabbits hopping about the stage ! The aim was to make everything seem as real as possible.

A Scene designed by Loutherbourg : A fight on a mountain pass

The number of theatres in London increased, and actors began to take their plays on tour to theatres that had been built in some of the important towns and cities in the country. In the nineteenth century both rich and poor could count playgoing among their pleasures.

Kean's setting for " A Midsummer Night's Dream "

The audience in the " gods "

The rich sat in the stalls and boxes, while those of more modest means were nearer to " heaven " in the upper galleries known as the " gods ", so called because they were close to the ceiling, which was decorated with paintings of gods and goddesses.

Visiting the theatre was not approved of by all classes of society. Nor did everyone consider that actors and actresses, however famous, followed a very praiseworthy occupation. The middle-class business men and shopkeepers thought of playgoing as a rather daring, even unpleasant, venture. Queen Victoria was a very infrequent visitor to the theatre, except on State occasions.

MUSIC HALLS

Working - class folk enjoyed an evening out at a " Music Hall ". This was a small theatre often adjoining a public house. Here they could forget their worries and join in the choruses of songs sung with tremendous rhythm and vigour by the artists on the stage.

In one show there might be twenty or more different performers—each with their own well-known acts or " turns ".

The " Chairman "

A typical Music Hall

Some, dressed in outlandish costumes, sang comic verses about sea bathing (a very new occupation!) motor - cars that would not go, mothers-in-law, and kippers. Others had serious songs about the brave soldiers and sailors fighting far away from home. Many sang patriotic songs about the greatness of the British Empire.

The singers were accompanied by a small orchestra of noisy brass instruments and drums, and were announced by the " Chairman " who introduced each act with a smart rap of his wooden mallet.

In between the singing acts, dancing, acrobatic and juggling turns enchanted the watchers. The feeling of gaiety made the Music Hall a place where you could forget the drudgery of long hours in a smelly factory, the cramped and dingy houses in the narrow streets of the ever-growing cities. There, among your friends you could sing, or laugh and drink, to your heart's content, or until your money ran out.

Three music-hall performers

Watching a Punch and Judy Show

5. THE " COMMEDIA DELL' ARTE "

ITALIAN TRAVELLING PLAYERS

Every year at the seaside on a bright summer's afternoon an excited audience of children gathers in front of a gaily striped tent to watch a Punch and Judy Show. There is Punch beating his poor wife, and tossing the baby into the audience. Despite all his wickedness, Punch always manages to escape the hangman's rope.

Strange as it may seem, the story of this hunchbacked old man goes back several hundred years to Italy in the sixteenth century. Then Punch or " Pulcinella " was not a puppet, but one of the characters in a rather special kind of play performed by acting troupes known as the " Commedia dell' Arte ".

Nowadays an actor learns the words of a play from a book, but the Commedia dell' Arte actors were only given a very brief outline of the play by the manager. They had to make up or " improvise " their own words.

This was not quite so difficult as it sounds. A player acting the rôle of a proud, rather vain soldier would keep that part in every play. He would learn a lot of boastful, noisy speeches, and so skilled was he at making jokes or witty remarks that he could always find something to fit the plot of any play that he was in. Even so he needed to be clever and quick-thinking. " Commedia dell' Arte " means " Comedy of the professional actor ".

These troupes were in great demand as they travelled through the cities and towns of Europe. One day they might entertain a nobleman at his mansion, on another, they would perform in a town hall or outside in the square.

A Punch mask

A troupe of Italian players of the " Commedia dell' Arte "

These cheerful bands of actors, and dancers, jugglers and acrobats, carried their baggage with them. They had a portable stage, and baskets loaded with bright costumes, strange masks and musical instruments. It did not take them very long to put up their stage, don their costumes and begin acting to the crowd who would very quickly gather.

King Henry III of France enjoyed seeing these actors so much that once he even paid a ransom for them when they had been captured by hostile foreigners.

Imagine for a moment that we are nobles at King Henry's court where a performance by these Italian actors is just beginning.

A street performance of the " Commedia dell' Arte "

Harlequin   *Columbine*   *Pantaloon*   *Capitano*   *Dottore*

Everyone is gathered in the great hall. First a minstrel sings a lilting folksong. As he withdraws the hero and heroine enter. The handsome young courtier wants to marry the beautiful young lady, but her father, " Pantaloon ", forbids it. His daughter is promised to somebody else. He stamps about the stage waving and shouting. What a comical figure he is, in a long black cloak, red vest, curling Turkish slippers, and with the top half of his face hidden by a mask !

Now there is a short interval or " lazzi ". We are entertained by an exciting acrobatic display. One of the tumblers holding a full glass of wine in his hand, turns a full somersault without spilling a drop.

Punch

King Henry III of France watches a performance of the " Commedia dell' Arte "

Brighella

*Harlequin squirts
water over Pantaloon*

HARLEQUIN AND COLUMBINE

The story continues. The young lady plots with "Columbine" her pretty, sharp-witted serving maid and a cunning rascal called "Arrlechio" (Harlequin). He dances on to the stage dressed in chequered coat and trousers flourishing a wooden sword, his mischievous eyes twinkling through the slits of his black mask. He is joined by two evil companions "Brighella" and "Pulcinella" (our old friend Punch).

As the three plot together Brighella strokes his sharp dagger. There is danger ahead for someone! But what is happening? The plotting has turned into a comedy act, with the comedians falling and tripping over one another. They are behaving very much like the "knock-about" clowns you see at the circus.

Meanwhile Pantaloon has gone to consult his friend, the "Dottore", a professor with a short grey beard, red cheeks and a flowing, black cloak.

These two foolish old men plan to outwit the lovers when the brave boastful "Capitano" (Captain) enters. What a grand figure he is with his enormous black moustache! No one dare defy the brave Capitano.

But it is all vain boasting. As Harlequin appears, the Captain dashes for safety behind the two old men.

At last, however, the lovers are united and the play ends with more acrobatics and dancing.

ENGLISH PANTOMIME

We must also thank the Commedia dell' Arte for the beginning of English Pantomime. So popular were the Italians when they visited England, that English actors borrowed their ideas. One famous Harlequin was John Rich, who acted the part without speaking.

From then, the plays became " Dumb Shows ". There were still plenty of jokes and tricks. The mischievous Harlequin often carried a magic bat. When he was in an awkward spot, he could rap his bat, and immediately change into someone else. The rap might also be a sign for the whole scene to be magically transformed.

An English Harlequin and Columbine

The English audiences enjoyed these " Harlequinades " so much that instead of being short " after - pieces " following the main play, they became entertainments on their own. Usually Pantaloon was an angry father pursuing Harlequin and Columbine who tried to escape him so that they could get married. Harlequin, as full of tricks as ever,

Pantaloon Columbine and the clown in an English Harlequinade

The Transformation Scene in " Cinderella "

played all kinds of practical jokes on Pantaloon.

Often a clown was mixed up in the fun, and a famous actor named Grimaldi made the clown's part the chief one in the Harlequinade. Pantaloon became a rather simple-minded assistant who was often in trouble.

The clown was never out of mischief. He did not mind taking something from a shop without paying, because it was always Pantaloon who was caught in the act by a Policeman. All kinds of tricks were used to keep the audience laughing. Pots of paste were flung about or tipped over unsuspecting victims. Turnips and cabbages sailed about the stage during mock battles.

Sometimes fairy tales were used to provide the stories, and the curious custom arose of an actress playing the part of the Principal Boy. At the same time, parts like Widow Twankey in *Aladdin* or the Ugly Sisters in *Cinderella*, were played by Music Hall comedians. They made the fun fast and furious.

Specially popular were the transformation scenes like the one in *Cinderella* where Cinders' pumpkin was changed into a wonderful coach with a swish of the Fairy Godmother's magic wand.

Pantomimes gradually became very much like the pantomimes we can see today, except that popular songs are now fitted into the story, as well as conjuring acts, tap dancing and other odd items.

The latest novelty is for a Pantomime to be performed " on ice ".

The Ballroom Scene from " Cinderella on Ice "

The audience sit on three sides of a large ice rink with the performers in the arena. The story takes second place to the skating display. Swirling skaters, in glittering costumes, weave and spin in intricate patterns, while coloured floodlights bathe them in a glow of blue, green, or any colour you could mention.

Although the ice provides plenty of slip-ups for the " Dame ", some of the real Pantomime comedy is lost. Because of the distance, the actors' voices have to be " dubbed " (spoken by someone else at a microphone). This prevents the comedians cracking jokes or making fun with the audience in the way that they do in the theatre.

Not many Pantomimes are per-formed in London theatres, but they are still popular in other parts of the country. Perhaps when you gaze with delight at a wonderful transformation scene or laugh at the antics of the Pantomime Dame on your next visit to the theatre, you will remember how it all began with those wandering Italian players of the " Commedia dell' Arte "

Arthur Askey as " Dame Martha " in " Robinson Crusoe "

6. THE MODERN THEATRE

GAS AND ELECTRICITY

On September 6th 1817, the Lyceum Theatre in London triumphantly announced " The Gas Lights will this Evening be introduced over the whole Stage ". A revolution in stage lighting was taking place. No longer were the actors lit by hundreds of flickering candles or oil lamps. Now, brightly burning gas jets illuminated them.

More important, a stage assistant sitting in the " wings " could alter the brightness of the flame by adjusting numerous taps and handles on the " gas table " to which all the pipes were connected.

A famous actor and theatre manager named Henry Irving tried all kinds of experiments to use this exciting new discovery properly.

First he made the audience sit in darkness. Until then, the auditorium (where the audience sat) had been as brightly lit as the stage. Then he placed small, coloured silk screens in front of the burners which softened the glare.

An actor in limelight

Perhaps you have heard the expression " being in the limelight ". This goes back to the days when a gas made from calcium (lime) was burnt to make a specially bright spotlight, much brighter than coal-gas. An actor standing in the limelight stood out among his fellow actors.

About sixty years later electricity was introduced into the theatre. Owners were very glad to change over because gas had been extremely dangerous. Now, long rows or " battens " of electric bulbs splashed the stage in light. Special " floodlights " gave extra brilliance where needed.

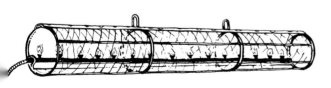

A gas batten

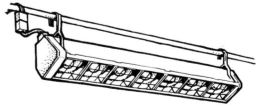

An electricity batten

Electrician's switchboard

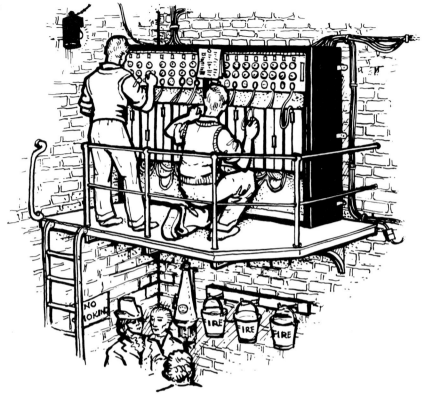

"Spotlights" could pick out a single place on the stage leaving everywhere else in complete darkness. With the use of instruments called "dimmers", lamps could be faded out or made brighter.

All the colours of the rainbow could be obtained by placing transparent sheets of coloured gelatine called "jellies" in front of the lamps. Perhaps you have seen wonderful lighting effects on your visits to the theatre. You can guess how much more marvellous the new lighting must have seemed, when it was first introduced.

Floodlight

Gelatine frames

Spotlight

GEORGE BERNARD SHAW

At the beginning of this century, an angry young Irishman, George Bernard Shaw, was busy writing plays. When these were produced, there was a great uproar, and Mr. Shaw was called all kinds of rude names. In fact, theatres were forbidden to perform the plays to the general public.

Yet when Shaw died in 1950, he was famed and respected throughout the world. You may wonder how this happened. Bernard Shaw wrote plays, not just to amuse people, but to show them some of the evil things that were happening.

He wrote about poor folk in dirty rat-ridden slum houses. He wanted people to realise how dreadful war was. At first, no one wanted to be reminded of these evils, but later on people realised the truth of what he said.

*George Bernard Shaw in 1905,
aged forty-nine*

Mr. Shaw's most famous play was *St. Joan,* which described how the poor peasant Joan of Arc led the French army to great victories, and restored the French king to his throne. It told also of her trial and death at the stake.

The trial of Saint Joan

The stage set of " The Lady's Not for Burning " by Christopher Fry

For those in gayer mood, there were spectacular musical plays like *Chu Chin Chow* which was performed more than two thousand times. The audience were enchanted by splendid singing and dancing, tuneful music, and marvellous oriental costumes.

The Drury Lane Theatre has been the home of many musical plays, often American. A famous one, *My Fair Lady* was, curiously enough, made from one of Bernard Shaw's plays. The story describes how a young Cockney girl was trained to talk and behave like a Duchess.

THE THEATRE TODAY

What would William Shakespeare or Samuel Pepys think if they paid a visit to present-day London ? How amazed they would be to learn that there are over forty theatres, and to find such a great variety of plays being performed—tragedies, comedies, musical plays. Some have delightful costumes and realistic scenery, others are acted on bare stages with a few plain blocks. They would hear of theatres where the same play has been running for two or three years.

No doubt Mr. Shakespeare would

be delighted to visit the Royal Shakespeare Company at the Aldwych Theatre. There he would see his own plays such as *Hamlet* and *Henry V* still being acted. He would also be able to share the worry and excitement of playwrights whose plays were being performed for the very first time. As they were waiting anxiously to hear how the audience enjoyed the new play, Mr. Shakespeare would remember the approving shouts that greeted his new plays at the " Globe " Theatre.

Not far away from the site of the

*Laurence Olivier,
first director of
The National Theatre
acting in Othello.*

" Globe " on the south bank of the Thames, William would also find his plays being performed at The National Theatre. This very special company of actors tries to present plays of which the whole country can be proud. Part of the money to pay for this theatre is provided by the Government. The rest is given by all kinds of well-wishers. The best plays that have ever been written by both English and foreign playwrights are presented at The National Theatre.

If Mr. Pepys visited the present Theatre Royal, Drury Lane, he would marvel at the many changes. Powerful electric floodlights and rows of spotlights have replaced the chandeliers of burning candles. Strong hydraulic lifts are now used to raise and lower parts of the stage. Even the curtains are operated by electric power.

The up to date stage lighting system at Her Majesty's Theatre, London (Strand Electric, London).

The " apron " stage of the Chichester Festival Theatre.

In the dressing rooms, Mr. Pepys would be intrigued to watch the actors applying " make-up " to their faces. He would see them using sticks or tubes of coloured grease which they smooth over their faces ; then carefully outlining their eyes and eyebrows and shading their cheeks and foreheads, so that they will look natural in the bright glare of the stage lights. Some might be sticking on false beards made of artificial " crepe hair ".

Both the visitors would observe that the larger audiences were very much quieter and better behaved than in their day. Shakespeare would be glad to see that the gallants no longer cluttered up the stage. Mr. Pepys would notice that the audience had come to see the play rather than to chatter among their friends or show off their fine clothes.

OTHER THEATRES IN BRITAIN

In other parts of Britain, several fine new playhouses have been built. Plays for young and adult audiences are performed. Clubs attached to the companies encourage young folk to find out more about the theatre. They can learn some of the secrets of " back-stage ", act and even try play writing.

You will remember that Shakespeare's " Globe " Theatre had an " apron " stage jutting out into the audience with spectators sitting on three sides. Modern designers have used this shape in planning new theatres such as the one at Chichester. Some plays are acted " in the round ". Here the actors are completely surrounded by the audience rather like the arena at the Circus.

REPERTORY THEATRES

In certain towns and cities you will find "repertory" theatres presenting a different play every week or fortnight. The actors in these companies work extremely hard, for while they are appearing in one play, they are busy rehearsing for the next one.

Here is the Belgrade Theatre, Coventry.

Much of the beautiful wood used in its construction has been presented by the people of Yugoslavia who wished to honour the bravery of the citizens of Coventry in the Second World War.

AMATEUR ACTORS

All over the country are groups of amateur actors who rehearse and present plays during their spare time. The luckier ones may be able to perform in a proper theatre, but most have to use church halls, schools or even converted barns! One that attracts many visitors is the "Maddermarket" in Norwich which has a stage very much like the one we saw in the Elizabethan theatres.

Maddermarket Theatre, Norwich

Perhaps your own school becomes a " theatre " at times. Indeed you may have joined in the hustle and bustle of rehearsal, despairing of ever learning your words. Your mother may have tirelessly shaped and sewed costumes, while teachers balanced on step-ladders, set curtains and fixed up the stage lighting.

At the last moment, grown-ups and children alike paint or stitch, hammer or screw, so that when the great day comes all is ready for the show to begin.

Whether you acted or helped behind the scenes, you have helped to continue " The Story of the Theatre ". As long as actors, writers and scenic artists keep on

Boys make scenery for a school stage

acting, writing or painting, and an eager audience gathers on the other side of the curtain, the story will never end.

The National Theatre on the South Bank of the River Thames, London

*John Gielgud
as Leontes in
" A Winter's
Tale "*

7. THE TELEVISION THEATRE

The wonder of television can bring the theatre right into our own home. A darkened living-room becomes the auditorium, while hundreds of miles away from this unseen audience, the actors perform in front of the magic eye of the television camera.

THE TELEVISION STUDIO

Have you wondered what it is like inside a television studio when a play is being presented? Let us take a peep behind the door that tells us firmly to KEEP OUT.

The studio is rather like a large hall, but one in a very great muddle. The whole space seems crammed with equipment—cameras, lights, long jointed poles carrying dangling microphones, and hundreds of pieces of scenery—all being fussed over by busy technicians and their assistants.

First to take our eye are the large cameras mounted on trolleys known

as "dollys" which allow the cameras to be moved smoothly and quietly about. Some dollys are almost like little cranes, and they can move the cameraman and his camera high up into the air, or swing him from side to side. Snaking away across the floor from each camera is a thick power cable like a

A Television camera

A Television Studio

hose pipe, which transmits the picture being taken by the camera.

The stage hands and " property " men are putting the finishing touches to the scenes, or " sets ", that have been built in the studio.

A technician adjusts the long pole or " boom " carrying a microphone that is suspended over the actors' heads. Great care must be taken to keep the microphones near to the actors but out of sight of the viewers.

The photograph above was taken during a performance of a play. Two rooms are seen, a sick-room and a sitting-room. You will notice that only a part of each room is shown. The sets are brightly lit by floodlights. The bright hot glare of these lights makes the actors' skins look pale and

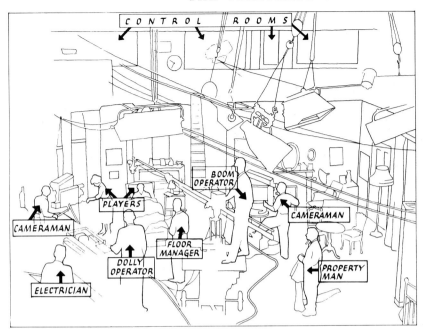

A key to the figures in the photographs on the opposite page

causes them to perspire, so their faces have been heavily " made-up " and powdered by the " make-up " girls. The drawing above shows you who some of the technicians are.

High above this scene of bustle and preparation, sitting in a sound-proof, glass-sided gallery, is the man in charge. He is the producer. In front of him is a row of television screens which show him the pictures being " shot " by the different cameras.

Also in the gallery are engineers who control the pictures being transmitted, the lighting, and sound effects produced by gramophone records. You notice that almost everyone except the actors wear

headphones with long trailing wires that occasionally get caught up in the equipment. The producer is able to talk to the cameramen and technicians in the studio below through these headphones without the sound being heard by viewers at home.

The Control room

The actors prepare for their performance before the television cameras

As time for transmission draws near, everyone feels tense and nervous. Actors hurry from their dressing-rooms, and the technicians set their machines working.

In the control gallery, the producer watches the final scenes of the programme before him. At the exact moment, he speaks into his microphone and the play begins. Then he stares at the row of screens, now and then ordering an alteration to sound or adjustment of cameras. Below in the main studio silence reigns, broken only by the voices of the actors who are hemmed in by a barricade of cameras, lights and microphones.

Some plays contain outdoor scenes which have been specially filmed beforehand. These are projected on to a cinema screen. Skilful engineers control these pictures so that they fit exactly into the play.

You may see an actor looking out of a window at a wonderful range of snow - capped mountains, or watching a scene in a busy factory workshop. It is quite impossible to have real mountains or factories in the studio, so these views are filmed and then shown on a screen just outside the window through which the actor is looking. This is called "back projection". Many other clever devices are used to make the pictures you see look realistic.

Back projection. The house behind the actors has been built up in the studio. The view of a street is being projected on to a screen

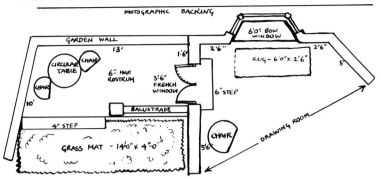

The designer's plan for the sets

THE PRODUCTION OF A TELEVISION PLAY

Preparation for the play begins several months before it is actually presented. First the writer discusses his story with the producer. Then an artist known as the "Designer" makes plans of the different sets needed, taking care to give the exact measurements of the doors, windows, etc., and how they are to be painted.

The carpenters and scenic artists set to work to build these sets, using light wooden frames covered with "papier maché" (a light, extremely strong kind of cardboard). On the day of the performance, all the bits and pieces are fitted up in the studio.

Only the parts of the room that appear before the cameras are constructed, so some of the sets look

The completed sets

rather strange. You may see steps that lead nowhere, or walls that cease abruptly just above the level of the doors.

Because the studios are used every day, the producer and his actors have to rehearse their play somewhere else. They may use a special rehearsal room or even an empty church hall. The studio manager chalks out a plan of the seats on the floor, and places a few plain wooden chairs to represent the beautiful armchairs and settees which will be used in the actual performance. Here the actors practise their parts until they are quite certain of their words and movements.

As well as working with the actors, the producer has to plan where the cameras are to be placed, and the kind of shots they have to take. He

A " close-up " of the three weird sisters in " Macbeth "

may want the camera within a few inches of the actor's face to get a close-up view of the angry villain, or he might want a long-distance view.

The engineers also have a special apparatus for gradually " fading out " one picture and " fading in " another. This is called " mixing ".

A performance of " Richard of Bordeaux "

All this planning and preparation keeps everyone extremely busy until the moment that the final scene fades away.

Whatever the difficulties, the show must go on. With so little time, the actors seldom have time to rehearse more than once or twice in the studio. Perhaps a camera breaks down during the performance, or a piece of scenery does not fit as it should. Sometimes the producer marvels that the play ever appears on the screen at all.

But this bustle and worry is hidden from us sitting quietly in our own homes. We cannot see the intent cameramen, the "boom" operators, or the watchful engineers in the gallery. Our small screen shows only what the producer wants us to see. We sit back and enjoy the performance brought to us in a way that would doubtless cause Mr. William Shakespeare and Mr. Samuel Pepys to stare in wonder at the "magic box" and the marvels it reveals.

On the television screen the plays we see relayed from the studio may be plays which were first acted in a theatre in Ancient Greece, or in the streets of a mediaeval city or in the Globe Theatre itself, all before an eager crowd of onlookers.

All through the centuries the theatre has had a magic attraction. Perhaps you have felt the magic yourself. If you have, then you can go on to discover the theatre for yourself. You may want to act, or to paint scenery, or to make costumes, or to write plays, or just go to see plays. Whichever you do, it will prove an exciting undertaking.

A Greek theatre built in the fourth century B.C.

GOING TO THE THEATRE

When we sit at home and watch plays on television, it is worth remembering that most of the actors learned how to act in the living theatre. It is much more fun to go to a theatre, because in a way you are helping the actors, as you are taking part in the performance yourself. Your laughter and your applause help the actors to give a better performance.

You may go to see a play in a theatre in London, or in one of the theatres in a big town, or in a repertory theatre, or in the school hall. Wherever it is, we must remember that the play is the important thing.

When all the audience are in their seats the lights of the theatre begin to fade ; conversation dies away ; the music ceases. There is a brief moment of silence, the footlights before the curtain light up, and then up goes the curtain itself and the play begins. The magic of the theatre is at work again.

The Bear Garden and the " Globe " Theatre

ACKNOWLEDGMENTS

I am grateful to John Lawson for his helpful co-operation in preparing the drawings. I am also grateful to the following for their permission to reproduce photographs or engravings: the York Festival Society, page 24; Bertram Park, from the Mander and Mitcheson Theatre Collection, page 26; the Trustees of the Shakespeare Memorial Theatre, page 37; the Victoria and Albert Museum, page 53; Wembley Stadium Ltd., page 62 (a); Moss' Empires Ltd., page 62 (b); the Radio Times Hulton Picture Library, page 65 (a); the Mander and Mitcheson Theatre Collection, page 65 (b); Angus McBean, pages 66, 67 (a), 71; the Strand Electric & Engineering Co. Ltd., page 67 (b); Reg Wilson Photography, page 68; the Belgrade Theatre Trust Ltd., page 69 (a); the Maddermarket Theatre Trust Ltd., page 69 (b); the *Radio Times*, page 72; the British Broadcasting Association, pages 73, 74, 76 (a) and (b); The National Theatre Company, page 70.

The portrait of Shakespeare on page 36 appeared on the title-page of the first folio edition of Shakespeare's works. The cover photograph is from the Mermaid production of *Gulliver*.

*An Elizabethan
Pedlar*

*An Elizabethan
Orange-seller*

79

INDEX